Caravan Co

Also from Tiger of the Stripe

Recipes from the Straw Bale House
Seasonal vegetarian cooking with gluten- & dairy-free recipes

SARA DANIELS

ISBN 978-1-904799-56-6

Caravan Cooking
The Versatile Vegetarian

FAITH HANCOCK

Richmond

TIGER OF THE STRIPE

First published in 2013 by
Tiger of the Stripe
50 Albert Road
Richmond
Surrey TW10 6DP
United Kingdom

ISBN 978-1-904799-54-2

Designed and typeset by
Tiger of the Stripe
Printed by Lightning Source

Contents

Introduction

ANYONE WHO HAS lived in a caravan, been on holiday in one or travelled around in one will know the difficulties that can arise when it comes to cooking. The space is much smaller than the average kitchen and storage can be a real issue! Having lived in an old campervan, a yurt, small caravans and larger static vans, I know the problems that lack of space can cause, and have come up with many recipes – some that are adaptations of old favourites, some that are completely new – which are suitable to cook in any space you have available. This cook book has been written using a wide variety of inspiration: dishes adapted from other recipes, picked up from different places around the world on my travels-or in some cases completely made up, due to necessity or boredom! This book is ideal for anyone who loves to cook, and you don't have to live in a caravan to enjoy it.

As for the leftovers, when you have a tiny fridge-or no fridge at all-it can be hard to store them, so I have devised many ways to use up those leftovers in other delicious dishes – this book removes two problems: having a versatile and interesting diet even when cramped into a tiny kitchen, and inventive ways to use leftovers so you don't have to store them or throw them away.

In Britain, we throw away an estimated 4.4 million tonnes of food every year. This works out at nearly £500 a year, for the average family, that is being thrown in the dustbin.

What a waste of good resources! Having been brought up in a household where nothing was allowed to go to waste, I have always felt strongly about the amount of food that is thrown away.

It can be boring, however, to eat the same thing over and over again just because you happen to have enough left to feed a small army…

Fear not, intrepid reader! There is a solution – the simple phrase that is drummed into all our heads these days – Reduce, Reuse, Recycle. The good news is that with food, this is both easy and very rewarding.

Leftovers have evolved since your granny's time, and are no longer in the realm of cold, congealed food and miserable children sitting stubbornly in front of a meal that will be served over and over again until it is eaten. Leftovers can be delicious, glamorous, healthy, and fun.

This is a book for everyone. This book will inspire you whether your kitchen is the size of a mansion or a postage stamp; help you to use up your leftovers; give you new ideas of delicious meals that can be plucked from thin air, and stretch your food budget further – without compromising on taste or health.

All the recipes in the following pages can be recycled into other equally yummy dishes; follow the 'Leftovers Tip' at the bottom of each recipe for ideas of what to do with your leftovers. These are just guides however; soon you will be full of ideas of your own about how to turn the remains of one delicious meal into something completely different-and equally delicious!

One final note-all the recipes in these pages are vegetarian, but can be very easily adapted for meat eaters-simply add your favourite cut, or substitute meat for Quorn or Tofu.

Happy Cooking!!

Acknowledgements

A JOURNEY IS never undertaken alone, and there are many people who deserve a mention at this, the final step:

A huge and ongoing thank you to my parents, for all your love and support in everything I do.

To Mister Ken (Knight), thank you endlessly for all the help and opportunities you have given me.

Special thanks to Vicky 'Curly Sue' Simon, for enthusiasm, ideas, inspiration and a shared love of food and cooking. Also for the mammoth cookathon – I couldn't have done it without you!

Big thanks to Jake Leach for the photography, fun and friendship.

Thank you to Rachel Brown of Brown Ink for fixing the cover photo-I have said it before and will say it again, you are a genius!

Robyn Morris, thanks for believing in me and giving me the chance- and the encouragement – to be a writer.

To the rest of my fantastic family and wonderful friends – you are too many to list but thank you for always being there and being amazing. I love you all.

Last but by no means least, heartfelt thanks to Peter Danckwerts of Tiger of the Stripe publishers without whom none of this would have happened. Thank you for making my dream come true!

'If more of us valued food and cheer above hoarded gold,
it would be a much merrier world.'
J. R. R. Tolkein, *The Hobbit*

Starters

Vegetarian sushi with dipping sauce

Mushroom Pate

Humous with vegetable sticks

Spring rolls

Chilli Quorn Strips

Tomato Pate

Individual Red Onion And Goat's Cheese Tarts

Homemade Onion Bhajis

Comfrey Pakoras

Fried Haloumi

Stuffing Patties

To Begin at The Beginning

A GOOD STARTER can be a real life saver when it comes to having a truly delicious meal. It can take the ravenous edge off even the most rampant appetite, so that the main course can be savoured and enjoyed for its own sake-not just because the diner is starving hungry!

A starter can also be a small respite for the cook; a chance to sit and regroup for a few minutes while the main course is simmering away, and a little time to chat with friends as you all prepare for the delights of the main course to come.

Often a good starter can set the tone for the whole meal, and as long as you stick to simplicity and don't get your knickers in a twist then all should run smoothly.

You can use starters as tiny little palate warmers, or to show off your culinary skills much the way a composer will build the music of a concerto up slowly before the crashing finale of the piece-make your starters tantalising and delicious, so that everyone is impatiently awaiting the main course.

You can make an entirely themed three course meal, or you can mix and match with your food styles, keeping everybody guessing.

You can even make a starter serve as a main course-if you are serving just one or two people, or if you increase the quantities to make a larger meal.

The following recipes are easy and quick to prepare, and any leftovers from them can be turned into other meals-or just kept in the fridge and nibbled at the following day!

Cooking is such fun, why restrict it to one or two courses? Go wild, release your inner chef, and-most importantly of all-enjoy yourself.

Vegetarian Sushi with Dipping Sauce

Serves 4
4 Sheets of Sushi Nori Seaweed
1oz (25g) White Rice
1 Avocado
1 Large Carrot
1 Onion
½ Small Cabbage

Dipping Sauce
10 ml Soy Sauce
3 Garlic Cloves, crushed
1 Tsp Dried Chilli
½ Tsp Dried Ginger
1 Tsp Sugar

Cook the rice according to instructions, then set aside to cool. Mash the avocado with a little lemon juice to prevent discolouration. Finely chop the onion and cabbage, and cut the carrot into thin matchsticks. Lay out the first sheet of nori, and spread a thin layer of avocado over the sheet. Spread out a layer of rice over this, then lay a quarter of the shredded cabbage on top. Follow this with a sprinkling of chopped onion, then place the carrots in a line near the edge of the seaweed. Carefully roll the seaweed into a cigar shape, then set aside. Repeat with the remaining sheets of nori. When all the seaweed is stuffed and rolled, slice into 2 inch sections and arrange on a plate with the dipping sauce.

To make the sauce, simply combine all the ingredients, mix thoroughly, and serve.

Leftovers Tip: Use any leftover dipping sauce in place of soy sauce for stir fries, rice dishes and curries.

Mushroom Pâté

Brilliant for spreading on toast or sandwiches.

Leftover Mushroom Soup (p. 34)
6 oz (175g) Wholemeal Breadcrumbs
¼ pint (150 ml) Hot Water
½ Lemon
1 oz (25g) Fresh Yeast
1 Small Onion
Knob of Butter
Ground Nutmeg to taste
Salt & Pepper

Finely chop the onion and fry in the butter (you can add 1-2 garlic cloves at this stage, but I usually find there is already enough in the soup-it's up to you.) Add the soup, and stir till heated through.

Soak the breadcrumbs in the hot water, then add to the pan with the lemon juice. Cook over a low heat until there is no free liquid remaining. Off the heat, stir in the remaining ingredients and season to taste.

Spoon into a serving dish, cover and refrigerate until needed. As a starter, serve the pate spread on warm Ciabatta bread.

Humous with Vegetable Sticks

Serves 6
8oz (225g) Chick Peas*
Water
4 Garlic Cloves
3 Tbsp (45ml) Oil
Juice of 1 Lemon
1 Tbsp Peanut Butter
1 Tsp Paprika
Chopped Parsley
2 Large Carrots
4 Sticks of Celery
1 Cucumber
2 Peppers

Slice the carrot, celery, cucumber and peppers into thick sticks about 4 inches long. Set aside.

Put the chick peas in a pan, just covered with water, and bring to the boil. Cover and simmer for 30-40 minutes, adding more water if necessary. Set aside to cool. (If using tinned chickpeas then reduce the cooking time to 15 minutes). Finely chop the garlic and put this in a liquidiser along with the oil, peanut butter and lemon juice. Add half the chick peas along with their water, and blend into a smooth paste. Continue adding the chick peas until they are all blended. (You can add more water, oil or lemon juice if the mixture is too dry.) Season well, transfer to a serving dish and serve with the sliced vegetables.

Leftovers Tip: Use up any uneaten vegetable sticks in a salad or stir fry.

---

* If you are using dried chick peas, they will need to be soaked overnight before use.

Spring Rolls*

Serves 2
1 Packet Rice Paper Pancakes
Beansprouts
1 Carrot
1oz (25g) Peas
Sweet Chilli Sauce
Soy Sauce

Slice the carrot into matchsticks. Take the first pancake and soak in a tray of warm water until it is soft and transparent. Lay it on a damp tea towel and spread with chilli sauce. Place a small handful of beansprouts in the middle of the sheet, and lay few sliced carrot sticks on top with 1 Tbsp peas. Fold the top and bottom of the pancake in towards the middle, then the two remaining sides. Roll the pancake into a small sausage shape and set aside. Repeat with the remaining ingredients. Serve with a bowl of soy sauce for dipping.

---

* These can be served as above, or deep fried-just heat about an inch of oil in a heavy based pan on a high heat, carefully place the rolls in and cook until golden brown. Lift out of the oil on a slotted metal spoon and drain on kitchen paper.

Chilli Quorn Strips

Serves 2
6 oz (180g) Quorn fillets, cut into ½ inch wide strips
2 Spring Onions
2 Cloves of Garlic
Oil
1 Fresh Chilli
1 Tbsp Fresh Coriander
Knob of Ginger
1 Tbsp Lime Juice
1 Tsp Brown Sugar
Soy Sauce
Chinese Leaves

Chop the spring onions and garlic, and fry in oil for 3-4 minutes. Remove the seeds from the chilli and finely chop, then add to the pan. Peel and crush the ginger and add this along with the lime juice, sugar, soy sauce and chopped coriander.

Cook on a low heat until the mixture is slightly thickened and caramelised, then add the Quorn strips. Increase the heat and cook for 4-5 minutes, making sure that the Quorn is cooked through. Serve on a bed of shredded Chinese leaves.

Leftovers Tip: Use any leftovers from this dish in Thai Stir Fry (p. 55)

Tomato Pâté

10-15 Cherry Tomatoes (Adjust amounts if using leftover
Roast Tomato Soup - p. 30)
4oz (100g) Wholemeal Breadcrumbs
¼ pt (150 ml) Hot Water
2oz (50g) Butter or Margarine
1 Large Onion
2 Garlic Cloves
1 oz (25g) Fresh Yeast
1 Tbsp Basil
Salt and Pepper

Soak the breadcrumbs in hot water. Chop the onion and garlic, and sauté in the butter until transparent. Roughly chop the tomatoes and add them to the pan-add the RoastTomato Soup if using at this stage.

Cook for a further 1–2 minutes. Add the soaked bread and cook on a high heat, stirring until no liquid is left.

Remove from the heat, add remaining ingredients and season to taste. Mix well and place into a shallow dish, refrigerate until needed.

Red Onion and Goat's Cheese Tarts

Serves 4
Shortcrust Pastry (You can either buy it ready-made
or make your own)
2 Large Red Onions
2 oz (50g) Butter
4 oz (100g) Goats Cheese
1 Tsp Dried Thyme
1 Tsp Dried Dill
Pastry
4 oz (110g) Self Raising Flour
2 oz (50g) Soft Butter/Margarine
1 Tsp Brown Sugar
3-4 Tbsp Cold Water
1 Tbsp Oil

Place the flour and salt in a large bowl. Cut the fat into small pieces, then add to the bowl and rub in until the mixture resembles fine bread-crumbs.

Dissolve the sugar in the water and stir in the oil. Add enough of the liquid to the flour mix to make it form a ball, then turn onto a floured surface and knead for a few minutes until the dough is smooth. Wrap in clingfilm and place in the fridge for at least 20 minutes.

When the dough has "rested", roll it out on a floured surface and use it to line four 4 inch (20 cm) flan dishes. Prick it all over with a fork, then bake for 5-7 minutes until it is set and slightly crisp.

Meanwhile, slice the onions finely and place in a large pan with the butter. Cook on a medium heat, stirring constantly to prevent sticking.

When the onions have softened, add the herbs and turn the heat down low and allow to simmer for 10-15 minutes.

Divide the onion mixture between the tarts. Slice the goats cheese into rounds and place one or two rounds onto each. Place in a preheated oven for 20 minutes until the pastry is cooked and the cheese is melted.

Homemade Onion Bhajis

Serves 2–4
1 Large Onion
8 oz (200g) Chickpea Flour/Gram Flour
1 Tsp Baking Powder
1 Tsp Chilli Powder
½ Tsp Turmeric
½ Tsp Dried Cumin
½ Tsp Dried Coriander
100ml Water
750ml Oil

Heat the oil in a heavy based saucepan. Combine all the remaining ingredients except the onion and mix to make a firm batter.

Slice the onion and add it to the mix.

Drop spoonfuls of the batter into the hot oil, taking care not to allow them to touch as they will stick. Cook for 1-2 minutes until golden brown.

Drain on clean kitchen paper and serve with one of the Tzatziki Dip Variations (p. 87). You can also serve the Bhajis with Coconut Curry (p.54)

Comfrey Pakoras

Pick young, tender comfrey leaves for this recipe. If Comfrey is not readily available, use spinach instead but double the amount as spinach reduces considerably when cooked.

Serves 4
4 oz (125g) Gram Flour
2 Tsp Oil
1 Tsp Ground Cumin
1 Tsp Dried Chilli
½ Tsp Salt
150 ml Water
5 oz (150g) Comfrey
Oil

Place all the ingredients, except the comfrey or spinach, into a large bowl or food processor and combine well. Leave the batter to stand for half an hour.

Tear the leaves into small pieces and combine with the batter.

Heat the oil in a deep pan or wok. You will need enough to cover the bottom of the pan by 2-3 inches.

Carefully drop even sized spoonfuls of the mixture into the hot oil. Cook for 1-2 minutes on each side, taking care when turning the pakoras to avoid hot oil splashes.

Place on kitchen paper to remove excess oil, then serve with Tzatziki Dip (p. 87) and Marrow Chutney (p. 103).

Fried Haloumi

Serves 2
1 Packet Haloumi
1 Egg
1 oz (100g) Breadcrumbs
1 Tsp Cayenne Pepper
1 Tsp Parsley
1 Tbsp Oil

Slice the haloumi into ½ inch (1cm) thick slices. Beat the egg and place into a small dish. Place the breadcrumbs, herbs and spices and salt into another small dish.

Coat both sides of each haloumi slice in egg, then place in the breadcrumbs to coat evenly.

Heat the oil in a heavy based pan, then add the slices of haloumi. Cook on a high heat for 2-3 minutes on each side.

Serve with Sweet Chilli Sauce for dipping, and a small green salad.

Stuffing Patties

This recipe works best in conjunction with Marrow and Brie Layer (Page 67) as you can use the leftover marrow stuffing to make these delicious patties.

Serves 2
1 Small Onion
4 Cloves Garlic
3 oz (75g) Tomato Puree
½ Tsp Brown Sugar
1 Tbsp Soy Sauce
1 Tsp Dried Chilli
1 Tsp Dried Basil
3 oz (75g) Breadcrumbs
Water
Oil

Finely chop the onion and garlic. Heat the oil in a medium sized pan, then add the onion and garlic and cook on a low heat until soft.

Add the soy sauce and herbs, and stir for 1 minute. Stir in the tomato puree and sugar. Add the breadcrumbs and thoroughly mix-you can add a splash of water if the mix becomes too dry, though it should be stiff enough to maintain its shape.

Remove from the heat and allow to cool. With slightly floured hands, take a plum-sized amount of mix and shape it into a ball, then flatten to about 1 inch (2.5cm) thick. Repeat with the rest of the mixture.

In a heavy based frying pan, heat about a tablespoon of oil and place the round patties into the pan. Cook for 3-4 minutes on each side, then remove and place on kitchen paper to absorb any excess oil.

Serve on a bed of leaves, with a dollop of Tzatziki on top of each patty (p. 87).

Soups

Roast Tomato

Carrot, Coriander and Sesame

Curried Parsnip

Creamy Leek and Potato

Butternut Squash

French Onion

Salad Soup

Coconut, Quorn and Lemongrass

Mediterranean Vegetable

Mushroom

Celery and Watercress

Homemade Croutons

Soup For The Soul

WHO DOESN'T LOVE a good soup? Whether a thick hearty warming soup for winter or a chilled Gazpacho on a summer's day, soup always has been and always will be a wonderful staple food.

Many years ago, soups were used to build up the strength of invalids as well as being a set course at the dinner table. All of the following soups can be used in either of the above categories, being stuffed to bursting with vegetable goodness-as well as being delicious in their own right.

The really great thing about soup is that it is so versatile; pretty much anything can make a wonderful soup, with the right preparation and cooking, and the leftovers of many soups can be adapted to make other exciting meals.

You can include a soup as part of a dinner party menu; as a stand alone dish for cold evenings, or as a light healthy lunch.

Soups can be made in batches then frozen for a later date, or made for immediate consumption. Hot or cold, thin or thick, blended or un-blended-your soups can take you in any direction you like.

With a good soup you will always have the ability to produce a hot, delicious meal from just about anything; and by following these recipes you will always have the righteous feeling of being able to turn your leftover soups into other dishes, instead of tipping that last uneaten bit down the sink or into the dog's bowl!

Roast Tomato

You will see I have not included measurements for this classic recipe-the amounts used are based on how many people this soup is intended for. As a rough guide, one punnet of cherry tomatoes, and 3 cloves of garlic will make soup for two people.

Serves 2-4
Cherry Tomatoes
Garlic
Small Chopped Onion
Soy Sauce
Water
Oil

Place cherry tomatoes and chopped garlic into a heatproof dish. Drizzle with oil, and place into hot oven. Cook until skins have split, stirring occasionally to mix the ingredients together. Remove from heat, and set aside.

Fry the onion in a small amount of oil, until soft. Add the tomatoes, soy sauce and water, and simmer for 15-20 minutes. Season to taste. Serve with croutons and salad.

Leftovers Tip: This soup, because of the lack of milk, makes a wonderful base for pasta sauces (pp. 79, 81).

Carrot, Coriander and Sesame

This is a mild, sweet soup. The sesame seeds add texture.

Serves 2
4 Large Carrots
1 Onion
Small knob of Ginger
1 Pt (300ml) Vegetable Stock
2 Tbsps Sesame Seeds
Coriander

Chop the onion and garlic, and slice the carrots thinly. Fry the chopped onion in a large pan with the garlic and thinly sliced ginger until soft.

Add the carrots and stir for 1-2 minutes before adding the stock. Stir to mix the ingredients, then cover and simmer until the carrots are soft.

Add the sesame seeds, then simmer for 1 minute. Add the chopped or dried coriander, then allow to cool thoroughly before liquidising. Garnish with coriander leaves.

Curried Parsnip

A very simple soup, with a mild sweet flavour. The curry powder adds a little kick!

Serves 2-3
4 Large Parsnips
1 Onion
Oil
1 Pt (300ml) Vegetable Stock
1 Tbsp Mild Curry Powder
Soy Sauce
Milk
Coriander to taste

Chop the onion, and add to a large saucepan with the oil and fry until soft. Chop the parsnips and add to the pan with the curry powder. Stir vigorously to coat the vegetables, then add the stock and bring to the boil.

Reduce heat and simmer until parsnips are soft. Add a dash of soy sauce, then the coriander, and cool before blending.

Add the milk and reheat gently.

Creamy Leek and Potato

This is a mild soup which appeals to everybody.

Serves 4
2 Leeks
2 Large potatoes
1 Onion
2oz (50g) Butter
1 Pt Vegetable Stock
¼ Pt Double Cream
½ Pt Milk
1 Tsp Dried Mixed Herbs
Salt and Pepper

Chop the onion and fry in the butter for 1 minute. Slice the leek into rounds and chop the potatoes (you can peel them but I never bother-the skin will not detract from either the flavour or the appearance of the soup, and adds vitamins). Add these to the pan and sweat for 3-4 minutes. Add the vegetable stock and herbs, cover and simmer on a low heat for 15-20 minutes until the potatoes are soft.

Remove from the heat and cool before liquidising. Stir in the milk and cream, season to taste and reheat gently before serving.

Mushroom

This soup is very useful for using up mushrooms which are past their best. It is not the most attractive colour, but the taste makes up for this!

> *Serves 3–4*
> 1 Small Onion
> 1-2 Cloves of Garlic
> 1 lb (500g) Mushrooms
> 2oz (50g) Butter
> ¼ Pt Vegetable Stock
> 2 Tbsp Double Cream
> Dill
> Salt and Pepper

Chop the onion and garlic, and fry in the butter until soft. Add the chopped mushrooms and stir until their juices start to run.

Add stock a little at a time and simmer for 8-10 minutes. Add a pinch of salt and the chopped dill. Cool, then liquidise and stir in the double cream.

Garnish with dill and serve with crusty bread.

Leftovers Tip: Leftover mushroom soup makes a rich mushroom pate (p. 16)

Squash

A thick creamy soup with a mellow flavour.

Serves –4
1 Small Onion
1-2 Cloves Garlic
1 Butternut Squash (or leftover Roasted Squash)
Salt and Pepper
½ Pt (150ml) Milk
1 Pt (300ml) Vegetable Stock

Chop the onion and crush the garlic, then fry in a heavy saucepan until soft. Chop the squash and remove seeds and skin. Add the chopped squash and fry 1-2 minutes.

Add the stock, bring to the boil then simmer for 10-15 minutes until soft. Add salt and pepper to taste, then allow to cool before liquidising. Stir in the milk and reheat gently.

Serve with crusty bread.

French Onion with Croutons

This unblended soup is both attractive and very tasty. The cheese adds an interesting flavour and texture as it melts.

Serves 2–3
4 Medium Onions
2 Cloves Garlic
Dried Sage
1 Pt (300ml) Vegetable Stock
Butter/Margarine
Grated Cheddar Cheese
2 Tbsp Soy Sauce
1 Tbsp Oil
3-4 Slices of Bread
Seasoning

Chop the onion and garlic, and fry in the butter for 2-3 minutes. Add sage and soy sauce and stir briefly. Add the stock, bring to the boil then simmer for 15-20 minutes.

Remove from heat. Cool slightly, and serve with grated cheese and Homemade Croutons (p. 40), season to taste.

Leftovers Tip: Any leftovers from this soup can be added to Onion and Thyme Tart (p. 46)

Coconut, Leek and Quorn

Carnivores: you can use chicken breast instead of Quorn (cook chicken thoroughly first)

Serves 4 as Starter or 2 as Main
Oil
3 Cloves Garlic
½ inch piece of Ginger
2 Leeks
3 Quorn fillets
1 Pt (500 ml) Coconut Milk
750 ml Vegetable Stock
1 Stick Lemongrass
Chives

Finely chop the ginger and garlic. Slice the leek into rounds, and fry in oil with the garlic and ginger.

In a separate pan, shallow fry the Quorn fillets until cooked through. Add to the garlic and ginger, then stir in coconut milk and stock. Add crushed lemongrass and bring to the boil.

Simmer for 5-10 minutes, then remove the lemongrass and serve garnished with chives.

Leftovers Tip: Any leftover coconut soup can be added to Coconut Curry (p. 54)

Leftover Salad

The ultimate leftover recipe! Any leftover salad can be used, but take care that no fruit or dressing has been added as this will spoil the flavour.

Serves 2
1 Tbsp of Oil
1 Onion
1-2 Cloves Garlic
Salad

Chop the onion and garlic, and fry in the oil until soft. Add the salad and cook for 1-2 minutes.

Add the stock, cover and simmer for 10-15 minutes. Leave to cool then liquidise. Add salt and pepper to taste.

Mediterranean Vegetable*

Serves 4
1 Onion
1 Large Carrot
1 Red Pepper
1 Green Pepper
1 Yellow Pepper
10 Cherry Tomatoes
5 Mushrooms
3-4 Garlic Cloves
Oil
1 Pt (500ml) Vegetable Stock
1 Tsp Mixed herbs

Chop all the veg into chunks and roughly chop the garlic. Place all the ingredients in a baking tray and drizzle with oil. Roast in a pre heated oven on a low heat for 20 minutes or until the vegetables are soft.

Add the herbs and mix well. Place the vegetables into a liquidiser with the stock and blend until smooth.

Add salt and pepper to taste, serve with olive bread.

---

*   You can use leftover Mediterranean Vegetables (see p. 65) and make up the ingredients to the measurements above.

Celery and Watercress

Serves 2
1 Onion
1 Head of Celery (or leftover Sweet and Sour Celery-page)
1 Packet of Watercress
½ Tsp Cumin
½ Tsp Paprika
4 Tbsp Natural Yoghurt
Black Pepper

Chop the onion into small pieces, and fry in the butter until soft. Add the celery and cook for a further 3 minutes, then add the watercress.

Sweat all ingredients for 2 minutes, stirring constantly, then add vegetable stock and spices. Simmer for 5-10 minutes, the leave to cool before liquidising.

Stir in the yoghurt just before serving.

Homemade Croutons

A great use for stale bread!

Bread (4 slices will make enough croutons for 2 people)
Oil
Vegetable Bouillon
1-2 Tbsp Soy Sauce

Chop the bread into ½ inch cubes. Place into a baking tray and drizzle with oil. Add the soy sauce and a sprinkling of bouillon. Toss to combine ingredients, then bake on a low heat for 20 minutes, turning frequently. Serve with soup.

What's in a Main?

Onion and Thyme tart

Homemade Pizza

Stuffed Peppers

Vegetable Stew

Cheese and Onion Quiche

Baked Garlic Risotto

Filled Field Mushrooms

Coconut Curry

Thai Stir Fry

'Chicken' and Mushroom Puff Pastry Pie

Vegetable Crumble

Marrow and Brie Layer

What's in a Main?

THE MAIN DISH is the focal point of your meal. Whether it be a light as a feather soufflé, or a big stodgy stew, the main dish is what we all look forward to with relish and champing jaws. It should always be substantial enough for however many people it is being prepared for, and just filling enough without being too much.

(But don't worry if you've made too much of a particular dish; by now you will probably have guessed that in many cases you can recycle any leftovers from these recipes into other dishes)!

A main dish can be something that follows a starter for an intricate dinner party menu, or a single satisfying portion for one on a work night. You need something that can be prepared with ease so that when you come home exhausted from a long day's work, you can still eat a yummy healthy meal instead of just throwing something in the microwave.

Main dishes should also be interesting and tasty enough that you can serve them to friends or family or visitors-but without the added stress element of feeling like you cannot possibly throw together a feast at the last minute... Well now you can!

The following main dishes tick all the above boxes-they are all healthy and nutritious; some can be made from the leftovers of other dishes, and many can be used as a base for other dishes. Oh, and did I mention that they're all delicious?

Onion and Thyme Tart

Serves 4–6
6 Large Onions (3 if using Leftover Onion Soup)
3 oz (75g) Butter or Margarine
2 Tsp Dried Thyme
Salt and Pepper
9 oz (250g) Shortcrust Pastry
Pastry
4 oz (110g) Self Raising Flour
2 oz (50g) Soft Butter/Margarine
1 Tsp Brown Sugar
3-4 Tbsp Cold Water
1 Tbsp Oil

Place the flour and salt in a large bowl. Cut the fat into small pieces, then add to the bowl and rub in until the mixture resembles fine bread-crumbs.

Dissolve the sugar in the water and stir in the oil. Add enough of the liquid to the flour mix to make it form a ball, then turn onto a floured surface and knead for a few minutes until the dough is smooth. Wrap in clingfilm and place in the fridge for at least 20 minutes.

When the dough has "rested", roll it out on a floured surface and use it to line four 4 inch (20 cm) flan dishes. Prick it all over with a fork, then bake for 5-7 minutes until it is set and slightly crispy.

Peel and slice onions, and fry in 2 oz (50g) marge or butter. Stir until golden and soft. Add leftover Onion soup at this stage, if using. Increase the heat and stir continuously until sticky and glazed. Add the thyme and stir well.

Grease a 9 inch/23 cm flan tin, and line with pastry. Bake "blind" at Gas Mark 7/220C/425f for 10 minutes or until golden. Pour the onion mix into the pastry. This dish can be served hot or cold, and is very good with Garlic Potatoes and a green salad.

Homemade Pizza

The Italian's answer to what to do with leftovers! You can make the base yourself for a fully homemade pizza, or buy the bases separately (I won't tell!). Any leftover vegetables can be used on your pizza, the following is just a guide-once you see how easy and delicious it is, you will become adventurous with your pizzas. Enjoy!

Serves 1–2
8 oz (200 g) Strong White Flour
½ Tsp Salt
1 oz (25 g) Butter or Margarine
¼ pint (150 ml) Warm Water
½ oz (15 g) Fresh Yeast
1 Tin Tomato Puree
1 Onion
2 oz (50 g) Mushrooms
1 Pepper
Cherry Tomatoes
Sweetcorn
Grated Cheese
Mozzarella

For the base, sift together the flour and salt into a large bowl and rub in the fat. Make a well in the centre, and add the water and yeast. Blend together with a wooden spoon, then knead with your hands on a floured surface until the dough is smooth and elastic. Cover and leave in a warm place until doubled in size. Roll out the dough on a floured surface and place on a large baking tray. Bake in a pre heated oven for 5-10 minutes, until the surface is just set.

Spread the tomato paste over the base. Finely chop the onion and sprinkle onto the base. Slice the mushrooms and arrange over the onion. Slice the peppers and place on, and do the same with the tomatoes and sweetcorn. Cover with grated cheese and mozzarella, then bake at Gas Mark 8 (230 c/450 f) for 30-35 minutes.

Stuffed Peppers

Serves 2
2 large peppers
1 small onion
2 cloves garlic
4 oz (100g) rice (or leftover Baked Garlic Risotto)
1 stock cube
Fresh basil
1 oz (25g) grated cheese
Salt and Pepper
Oil

Remove the stalks and seeds from the peppers and score them lightly on either side. Place upright in a baking tray with 1-2 tablespoons of water.

Cook the rice (if using) according to instructions, then set aside. If you are using leftover Risotto, simply reheat the rice thoroughly.

In a medium saucepan, fry the chopped onion and garlic with a dash of oil. Add the stock cube and simmer until the onion is soft. Add the rice at this stage, stirring constantly to stop it from sticking. Add the basil and seasoning, stir to combine. Remove from the heat.

Preheat the oven to gas mark 5. Fill the peppers with the rice mixture, top with grated cheese and cook for 20-25 minutes, until the rice is melted and the peppers are softened but not squishy. Serve with any leftover rice.

Cheese and Onion Quiche

Serves 4

Pastry
4 oz (100g) Self Raising Flour
2 oz (50g) Soft Butter/Margarine
1 Tsp Brown Sugar
3-4 Tbsp Cold Water
1 Tbsp Oil

Filling
4 Large Eggs
¼ Pt Milk
8 oz (200g) Strong Cheddar Cheese
1 Onion
Salt and Pepper
Dried Mixed Herbs, Pinch

Place the flour and salt in a large bowl. Cut the fat into small pieces, then add to the bowl and rub in until the mixture resembles fine bread-crumbs.

Dissolve the sugar in the water and stir in the oil. Add enough of the liquid to the flour mix to make it form a ball, then turn onto a floured surface and knead for a few minutes until the dough is smooth. Wrap in clingfilm and place in the fridge for at least 20 minutes.

When the dough has 'rested', roll it out on a floured surface and use it to line four 4 inch (20 cm) flan dishes. Prick it all over with a fork, then bake for 5–7 minutes until it is set and slightly crisp.

While the pastry is in the oven, place the eggs and milk into a large bowl and beat until creamy. Grate the cheese and add, saving a handful to sprinkle over the top of the quiche. Season to taste. Finely chop the onion and sprinkle it over the pastry base. Carefully pour over the egg mixture (it can be a good idea to do this without removing the base from the oven, as carrying it around the kitchen can lead to spilling).

Bake in the preheated oven at Gas Mark 5 for 30-35 minutes, or until a knife inserted into the quiche comes out clean. About halfway through the cooking time, sprinkle the remaining cheese over the quiche.

Leftovers Tip: Any leftover quiche is great for a light lunch, served with a green salad. Turn any leftover pastry into dumplings by rolling into balls and adding to Vegetable Stew (p. 51) for the last 20 minutes of cooking time.

Vegetable Stew

A hearty winter staple to keep your cockles warm! You can use any veg you like for a stew, but due to the long cooking time it is best to use a majority of root vegetables.

Serves 4–6
2 Potatoes
2 Carrots
2 Parsnips
1 Swede
1 Large Onion
1 Tin Tomatoes
1 ½ -2 Pt Vegetable stock
1 Tsp Each: Dried Basil, Dried Rosemary, Dried herbs
1 Bay Leaf

Chop all the root vegetables – you can peel them all if you like, but I tend to leave the skins on carrots, potatoes and parsnips for the added nutrients and flavour.

Chop the onion and place into a deep, heavy saucepan with a knob of butter. Fry until soft, then add the remaining ingredients.

Turn to a very low heat and simmer for 1–2 hours, stirring occasionally.

Leftovers Tip: Add leftover stew to Mediterranean Vegetable Soup (p. 39)

Baked Garlic Risotto

Serves 4
8 oz (250 g) Arborio (risotto) Rice
2 Tbsp Oil
1 Whole Garlic Bulb
1 Onion
2 Celery Stalks
1 Red Pepper
2 oz (50 g) Frozen Peas
2 oz Mushrooms
1 Tsp Dried Oregano
1 Tsp Dried Dill
1 ½ pint (900 ml) Vegetable Stock

Heat the oil in a large, heavy based saucepan or wok. Add the rice and stir for 5 minutes.

Chop the celery, pepper and mushrooms and add to the pan. Cook for 3-4 minutes before adding the stock and herbs. Simmer for 5 minutes.

Place the rice into a large baking dish, placing the whole garlic in the middle. (Alternatively, you can separate the cloves and scatter them throughout the dish, stirring well to mix).

Cover with foil and cook in a preheated oven for 25-30 minutes until the rice is soft. Garnish with fresh parsley and serve.

Leftovers Tip: Use up uneaten Risotto in Stuffed Peppers (p. 48), or Congee (p. 74)

Filled Field Mushrooms

Serves 4
4 Large Flat Mushrooms
1 Small Onion
2-3 Cloves Garlic
1 Vegetable Stock Cube
2 Tbsp Frozen Peas
8 oz (200g) Breadcrumbs
1 Tsp Dried Dill
1 Tsp Mixed Herbs
½ Tsp Cayenne Pepper
Ground Black Pepper
Butter
Oil
Water

Remove the stalks from the mushrooms and set aside. Place the mushrooms, flat side down, on a baking dray and dab a small amount of butter in the centre on each (this will help keep the mushrooms moist during cooking).

Chop the onion, garlic and mushrooms stalks finely and place in a small pan with the oil over a medium heat. Cook for 2 minutes, until the onion is soft but not brown.

Add the stock cube and a splash of water to help dissolve it. Cook, stirring constantly, for another 2 minutes before adding the herbs and cayenne pepper.

Turn the heat down to a simmer and stir in the breadcrumbs and frozen peas. Add black pepper to taste, then remove from the heat.

Share the stuffing mix evenly over the mushrooms, and bake in a preheated oven on a medium heat for 20 minutes, or until the mushroom juices start to run. Serve with a green salad and baked potatoes.

Leftovers Tip: Use any leftover mushroom stuffing as a base for Stuffed Peppers (p. 48).

Coconut Curry

Serves 4
2 Large Red Chillies
1 Small Onion
2 Garlic Cloves
1 Inch Piece Fresh Ginger
Fresh Basil
Fresh Coriander
1 Lime
1 lb (500g) Sweet Potato
1 Head of Broccoli
1 Large Carrot
4 oz (100g) Fine Green Beans
14 Fl oz (400 ml) Can Coconut Milk
Soy Sauce
1 Tbsp Brown Sugar

Place the first seven ingredients into a food processer and blend until smooth.

Without shaking the can of coconut milk, spoon the first layer into a deep frying pan or wok, and cook over a medium heat until thickened and reduced by about half.

Stir in the spice mix and cook, stirring, for 3 minutes. Add the vegetables to the pan. Mix the remaining coconut milk with water in the tin, then pour over the vegetables with the soy sauce and sugar. Cook for 10-12 minutes, until the sweet potatoes are soft. Add chilli and herbs to taste, then serve with noodles or rice.

Thai Stir Fry

A deliciously simple dish, with the added bonus of being useful for using up any leftover veg! Meat eaters can add their choice of cooked meat – sliced chicken works best.

Serves 2
2-3 Cloves Garlic
1 Large Onion
Knob of Ginger
Fresh Chilli to Taste
2 Medium Carrots
1 Leek
Peppers (I like to use one of each colour)
1 Small Courgette
Baby Sweetcorn
Beansprouts
Mange Tout
2 Tbsp Soy Sauce
1 Tbsp Peanut Butter
1 Tbsp Brown Sugar
Juice of 1 Lime
Fresh Coriander
Fresh Basil

Slice the onion and finely chop the garlic and ginger. Slice all the remaining vegetables, except the sweetcorn, mange tout and beansprouts, into thin matchsticks. In a wok or heavy based saucepan, heat 1 Tbsp of oil over a high heat, and add the onions, garlic, ginger and soy sauce. Cook for 1 minute, then stir in the peanut butter, lime juice and sugar. Add the carrots and cook for a further 2 minutes. Add the finely chopped fresh herbs and chilli, adding more soy sauce if the vegetables are sticking. Add the remaining vegetables and cook for 2-3 minutes, stirring constantly to combine the flavours and prevent burning.

Serve on a bed of egg noodles.

Mushroom Stroganoff

Serves 4
4 oz (100 g) Chestnut Mushrooms
4 oz (100 g) Oyster Mushrooms
4 oz (100 g) Shiitake Mushrooms
4 Spring Onions
2 Cloves of Garlic
2 oz (50 g) Plain Flour
1 Tbsp Vegetable Bouillon
¼ pint (150 ml) Milk
4 Tbsp Double Cream
2 Tbsp White Wine
1 Tsp Parsley
1 Tsp Mixed Herbs

Chop the spring onions and garlic and cook for 1 minute with a splash of oil in a large pan. Add the flour and stir to make a paste, then add bouillon. Slowly stir in the milk, cream and herbs, and simmer until thickened.

Roughly chop the mushrooms and place in another pan with a small amount of water and bring quickly to the boil. Remove from the heat.

Stir the mushrooms and white wine into the cream mixture, adding the mushroom's cooking water if the mixture is too thick. Simmer for 1-2 minutes to allow the flavours to combine, then remove from the heat and serve on a bed of rice.

Leftovers Tip: Any uneaten Stroganoff can be added to "Chicken" and Mushroom Puff Pastry Pie (p. 57). Unused rice can be made into Congee (p. 74).

'Chicken' and Mushroom Puff Pastry Pie

Serves 4-6
1 Packet Puff Pastry
3 Quorn Fillets
8 oz (200 g) Mushrooms
1 Onion
2 Cloves of Garlic
2 Tbsp Plain Flour
½ pint Vegetable Stock
½ pint Milk
4 Tbsp Double Cream
1 Tsp Wholegrain Mustard
2 Tsp Parsley
1 Tsp Basil

Chop the onion and garlic and cook in a large saucepan with a splash of oil until soft. Chop the Quorn fillets into ½ inch (1 cm) pieces and add to the pan. Cook for 4-5 minutes on a low heat, stirring to prevent sticking.

Chop the mushrooms roughly and add to the pan with the wholegrain mustard and stir to coat. Remove from the heat and stir in the flour. Gradually add the stock and return to the heat, stir until thickened. Add the milk and simmer for 1 minute. Remove from the heat and stir in the cream and herbs.

Roll out the puff pastry on a lightly floured surface, then drape it over a baking tray. Place the filling in one half of the pastry and fold the other half over. Brush a little milk on the edge to help sealing, then press the edges together firmly. Lightly score the top with a knife to make vertical lines on the pastry, then brush with milk.

Cook in a preheated oven at Gas Mark 5 (190 c/375 f) for 30 minutes, or until golden brown. Serve with Spicy Courgette (p. 69), and Sweet 'n Sour Celery (p. 73).

Vegetable Crumble

Serves 4–6
1 Large Onion
2 Garlic Cloves
6 oz (150 g) Mushrooms
2 Large Carrots
1 Courgette
1 Leek
1 Red Pepper
14 fl oz (400 Ml) Vegetable Stock
2 oz (50 g) Plain Flour
4 Tbsp Double Cream
2 Tbsp Chopped Parsley
2 oz (50 g) Butter or Margarine

Topping
6 oz (200g) Plain Flour
4 oz (100g) Chopped Mixed Nuts
3 oz (75 g) Margarine
1 Tsp Dried Mixed Herbs
1 Tbsp Fennel Seeds

Slice all the vegetables. Place the mushrooms in a saucepan with the stock. Bring to the boil, then cover and simmer for 10 minutes. Drain and reserve the stock.

Chop the onion and garlic finely, and place in another saucepan with the butter or margarine over a medium heat. Cook until softened, then add the remaining vegetables and cook for a further minute. Stir in the flour.

Remove from the heat and slowly stir in the mushroom stock. Return to the heat and cook, stirring constantly, until thickened. Add the mushrooms, cream and parsley, then pour into an oven proof dish.

Mix the dry ingredients for the topping together, then mix in the margarine until the mixture resembles coarse breadcrumbs.

Cover the vegetables with the crumble mix, then sprinkle over the fennel seeds. Bake in a preheated oven at Gas Mark 5 (190 c/ 375 f) for 25-30 minutes until golden brown.

Serve with Honey Glazed Carrots (p. 70) and Balsamic Peas (p. 73).

Marrow and Brie Layer

Serves 4
1 Large Marrow
1 Small Onion
4 Cloves Garlic
3 oz (75g) Tomato Puree
½ Tsp Brown Sugar
1 Tbsp Soy Sauce
1 Tsp Dried Chilli
1 Tsp Dried Basil
3 oz (75g) Breadcrumbs
Water
Oil

Peel the marrow and remove the seeds. Slice into eight rings 1 inch (2.5 cm) thick and place in a foil lined baking tray with enough water to just cover the bottom.

Finely chop the onion and garlic. Heat the oil in a medium sized pan, then add the onion and garlic and cook on a low heat until soft.

Add the soy sauce and herbs, and stir for 1 minute. Stir in the tomato puree and sugar. Add the breadcrumbs and thoroughly mix-you can add a splash of water if the mix becomes too dry, though it should be stiff enough to maintain its shape.

Remove from the heat and allow to cool.

Fill four of the marrow rings with the stuffing mix, then slice the brie and lay it over the stuffing. Place the remaining four marrow rings on top of the four filled ones, then fill these with stuffing mix and add another layer of brie.

Bake in a preheated oven on Gas Mark 4 for 30-35 minutes, until the marrow is softened and the brie is melted.

Leftovers Tips: Use any leftover stuffing for Stuffing Patties (p. 25). Leftover marrow can be added to Coconut Curry (p. 54).

Optional Extras

Roasted Squash

Mediterranean Roasted Veg

Spuddy Wedges

Spiced Courgette

Glazed Carrots

Interesting steamed Greens

Braised Red Cabbage

Garlic Potatoes

Sweetcorn Surprise

Sweet N Sour Celery

Balsamic Peas

Congee

Optional Extras

So now you have created your masterpiece of a main, the burning question remains: What to serve it with?

It's all very well having a knockout main course, like a perfect pie or mind blowing melange of flavours-but if you don't have something to serve alongside it then it can feel a bit like the unfinished symphony. It's brilliant, but there's something missing…

Don't panic! The following pages will show you a few bits and pieces that are very easy and quick to prepare, and will complement whatever you are having as a main course.

Vegetables can be very exciting, and not just there to bulk up a meal or to remind you of your mum telling you to eat your greens. A good side dish can be really good, both in terms of taste and nutrition, and in terms of setting off the rest of your meal to perfection.

And it's not just vegetables! Follow my tips on what to do with your leftover rice and how to serve it as a side dish for other main meals.

Making sure your extras are as good as your main dish is a very important part of cooking; paying attention to the details will make such a difference to your finished product.

The following can be used in conjunction with main dishes, or as stand-alone small meals.

Roasted Squash

Oh so simple, and oh so good!

> *Serves 2-4*
> 1 Butternut Squash
> Oil
> Salt and Pepper

Cut the squash in half, remove the seeds and soft pith, then slice thickly. Place slices into baking tray, drizzle over the oil and seasoning, then bake in a pre-heated oven at gas mark 6 for 30-45 minutes or until soft.

Leftovers Tip: Leftover squash slices can be used in Squash Soup (p. 35)

Mediterranean Roasted Vegetables

This dish is not only delicious, but really pretty to look at thanks to the mix of colours.

Serves 4–6
2 Carrots
4 oz (100g) Mushrooms
1 Medium Sweet Potato
4 oz (100g) Broccoli Florets
1 Yellow Pepper
1 Red Pepper
10 Cherry Tomatoes
2 oz (50g) Green Beans or Mange Tout
1 Tbsp Dried Mixed Herbs
1 Tsp Basil
1 Tsp Paprika
Oil
Soy Sauce
Salt and Pepper

Peel the sweet potato and cut into chunks. Roughly chop the carrots and mushrooms, and slice all the remaining vegetables into strips. Place all the veg into a deep baking dish, and drizzle with enough oil so that they are all coated.

Add the remaining ingredients, stir to coat everything, then place into a preheated oven and cook at Gas Mark 6 for 20-30 minutes.

Leftovers Tip: Use any leftover veg in Mediterranean Vegetable Soup (p. 39). Also try to save the juices from the pan after cooking, as it makes a great base for stock and gravy.

Spuddy Wedges

A good substitute for chips, and very yummy!

> *Serves 3–4*
> 4 Large Potatoes
> Oil
> Soy Sauce
> 1 Stock cube
> Dried Chilli

Chop the potatoes into wedge shapes (leaving the skin on). Place into a baking tray, and drizzle over enough oil to thinly coat each wedge. Crumble over the stock cube, add soy sauce and chilli to taste, along with dried herbs of your choice. Cook in a pre-heated oven at gas mark 6 for 25-30 minutes, or until potatoes are soft.

Leftovers Tip: Leftover wedges are very versatile-add them to curries, stir fries or soups-or eat them cold the next day!

Strain the leftover oil from the potatoes, store in a jar and use as flavoured oil for other dishes such as Mediterranean Vegetables (p. 39).

Spiced Courgette

Especially good in summer, with small, sweet courgettes.

Serves 2
Oil
1 Red Chilli, deseeded and finely chopped
1 Small Onion
3 Garlic Cloves, crushed
Tomato Puree
Salt, Pinch
1 Tsp Brown Sugar
Soy Sauce
Fresh basil
2 Medium Courgettes
½ Tin Chopped Tomatoes

Put the first four ingredients into a saucepan and fry until soft. Stir in 2 tablespoons of tomato puree and a tablespoon of soy sauce. Add the salt, sugar and basil, then stir in the chopped tomatoes and cook until thickened. Chop the courgette and add to the pan, then cook until just soft.

Leftovers Tip: Leftovers from this dish can be used to bulk out pasta sauces such as Spaghetti Bolognese (p. 79).

Honey Glazed-Carrots

A carrot recipe that everyone will love! The splash of vodka gives the dish a slight lift.

Serves 2
4 Large Carrots
Knob of Butter
1 Tbsp Honey
1 Tbsp Brown Sugar
Salt and Pepper to taste
1 Tbsp of Vodka
Water

Chop the carrots into sticks about 3 inches long. Place in a saucepan with all the remaining ingredients, cover and simmer for 10-15 minutes or until carrots are soft.

Leftovers Tip: Leftover honey carrots can be added to carrot soup (Page 27) or added to curries or stir fries.

The cooking juices should be strained off and kept in the fridge-they make an excellent vegetarian dripping!

The juices can also be used as a base for Honey Glaze Gravy (p. 85).

Braised Red Cabbage

Serves 4
1 Whole Red Cabbage
1 Red Onion
2 Small Apples
7 Fl oz (200 ml) Malt Vinegar
2 Tbsp Brown Sugar
Splash of Red Wine

Finely chop the onion and sweat in a saucepan with a knob of butter until softened. Finely chop the cabbage and add to the pan, stirring well to coat. Core and chop the apples into small chunks and add to the pan. Stir in the vinegar and sugar, cook on a low heat for 10 minutes. Add the wine, turn up the heat and cook for a further 2-5 minutes until thickened.

Garlic Potatoes

An easy and simple recipe to use up leftover boiled potatoes.

Serves 2–4
Leftover Boiled Potatoes
Butter/Margarine
4-5 Cloves Garlic
Chives

Melt the butter or marge in a large saucepan. Crush the garlic and add to the pan, stirring well for 1-2 minutes. Roughly chop the potatoes into 1 inch pieces, and add to the pan. Stir well to coat the potatoes, then cook on a low heat until everything is heated through. Add chopped chives to taste, then serve.

Sweetcorn Surprise

The chilli adds the surprise element, so go carefully if you don't like it hot!

Serves 2–3
1 Tin Sweetcorn
1 Small Onion
Butter or Margarine
1 Tsp Dried Chilli
1 Tsp Brown Sugar
Squeeze of Lemon Juice

Chop the onion, then fry in the butter or marge until soft. Add the sweetcorn and the remaining ingredients, cook for 5 minutes until heated through.

Leftovers Tip: Leftovers from this side dish can be made into sweetcorn relish (p. 102).

You can also add it to a simple omelette, or a salad, or sprinkle it over your pizza. A very versatile side dish!

Sweet 'n Sour Celery

Serves 2–4
1 Tbsp Butter/Margarine
1 Head of Celery
1 Bay Leaf
½ Tbsp Soy Sauce
1 Tbsp White Wine Vinegar
½ Tbsp Brown Sugar
Dill

Melt the butter or margarine in a saucepan with the bay leaf. Chop the celery into diagonal pieces and add to the pan. Cook for 1 minute, stirring constantly, then add the remaining ingredients. Cover and simmer for 10-15 minutes, then serve. (Don't forget to remove the bay leaf!)

Leftovers Tip: Any leftovers from this side dish can be made into Celery and Watercress Soup (p. 40)

Balsamic Peas

Serves 2–3
1/2 Packet Frozen Peas
1 Tsp Wholegrain Mustard
3 Fl oz (100 ml) Balsamic Vinegar
1-2 Tbsp Sugar
1 Tsp Dried or Fresh Mint

Place all the ingredients into a small saucepan and heat, stirring continuously until mixed. Cook on a medium heat until the peas are cooked through. Season to taste.

Leftovers Tip: Save the juices from this dish and when cool you can use it in Salad Dressing (p. 87).

Congee

This incredibly simple Asian dish is very useful for using up any leftover rice-just always ensure that when reusing rice to heat it through thoroughly before serving.

Serves 2
6 oz (150g) Rice
Water
Soy Sauce
Herbs

Cook the rice according to instructions, or take your leftover rice and place into a pan. Cover with water and simmer on a low heat for 15-20 minutes. When the water has been absorbed add more to cover the rice, and continue to cook, adding more water where necessary, until the rice has a very soft, porridge like consistency (this may take up to an hour).

Add soy sauce and herbs to taste.

Serve as a filling side dish, best served with Naam Prick (p. 86).

Ooh, Saucy!

Spaghetti Bolognese

Blue Cheese and Pine Kernels

Sundried Tomato

Creamy Chestnut and Port

Red Onion Gravy

Simple White Sauce

Honey Glazed Gravy

Nam Prick

Simple Salad Dressing

Tzatziki

Ooh, Saucy!

I F YOU CAN make a good sauce, you can make anything. It's that simple! The subtle combinations of flavours and the varying thicknesses of your sauces are entirely up to you, but you should be aware that some sauces will turn out much thicker than others.

Your sauces can provide the base of your meal-in the case of pasta sauces especially-or they can be an exciting extra if you feel that a certain dish needs a little something.

It is always good to have a sauce or two up your sleeve; they are so versatile and can be turned from a fragrant gravy into a whole dish in moments-perfect for unexpected guests!

These sauces are all simple and easy to prepare, and you can really impress your friends by whipping up a delicious meal apparently out of nowhere.

Salad dressings are equally important, as they can turn the most bland and unexciting bunch of vegetables into an exotic dish of deliciousness!

Homemade sauces, to me, always taste far better than the packet stuff-and you have the added bonus of knowing exactly how much of what has gone into it. The majority of these sauces are low in salt, especially compared to packet sauces, which is good news for those of us who eat too much salt in our diet.

Go ahead-get in that kitchen and get saucy!

Spaghetti Bolognese

Serves 4
1 Large Onion
4 Cloves Garlic
1 Tsp Yeast Extract
1 Tin Tomatoes
4 large Fresh Tomatoes
1 Packet Vegetarian Mince
1-2 Tsp Dried Mixed Herbs
1 Tsp Fresh Basil
Salt, Pinch
1 Tsp Sugar

Finely chop the onion and garlic, and place into a pan with a dash of oil. Sweat over a low heat until softened, then add the yeast extract. Stir until blended and smooth, then add the mince and cook over a high heat for 2–3 minutes.

Chop the tomatoes and add to the pan, then add the tinned tomatoes. Turn down the heat and simmer for 10-15 minutes.

Add the remaining ingredients and cook for a further 5 minutes until the sauce has thickened.

Blue Cheese And Pine Kernel

Serves 2
2 oz (50g) Pine Kernels
8 oz (200g) Full Fat Cream Cheese
½ Pt (150ml) Milk
3 oz (75g) Blue Cheese
1 Tbsp Fresh Basil

Place the soft cheese and the milk into a saucepan and heat gently, stirring to mix. Stir in the blue cheese and basil, cook for a further 3-5 minutes until everything is blended and smooth.

Place the pine kernels on a baking sheet and grill until browned-this won't take long, so keep an eye on them and make sure they are turned regularly.

Stir the pine kernels into the sauce.

This dish is best served with steamed broccoli and mushrooms, all stirred through some nice al dente pasta.

Sundried Tomato

Serves 2
1 Small Onion
4 Garlic Cloves
8 oz (200g) Sundried Tomatoes
1 Tin Tomato Puree
Sugar, Pinch
Salt and Pepper

Chop the onion and garlic very finely, and place into a heavy based saucepan with a splash of oil. Cook gently while you finely chop the sundried tomatoes, then add these to the pan.

Add the tomato puree and cook over a high heat for 5 minutes, stirring constantly. When the sauce has thickened and reduced, lower the heat and stir in enough water to make a smooth consistency.

Add the seasonings and herbs.

Best served with a simple, well cooked pasta-just stir the sauce through before serving and add some Parmesan cheese.

Leftovers Tip: Any unused sundried tomato sauce can be used to bulk up Roast Tomato Soup (p. 30).

Creamy Port and Chestnut

This ridiculously decadent and yummy sauce is ideal for special occasions!

Serves 2 as Sauce, 4 as Gravy
1 Shallot
8 oz (200g) Cooked Chestnuts
½ Pt (150ml) Single Cream
2-3 Tbsp Vegetable Stock
5 Tbsp Port
Salt and Pepper

Finely chop the shallot and fry gently until soft. Mash the cooked chestnuts and add to the pan with the vegetable stock, then simmer on a low heat for 5 minutes.

Remove from the heat and stir in the cream, then slowly add the port. Return to the heat and cook on a medium heat for 2-3 minutes, until the sauce is reduced and thickened.*

---

*   If the sauce becomes too thick, simply add more vegetable stock and whisk until smooth.

Red Onion Gravy

Serves 4–6
2 Large Onions
1 oz (25g) Butter or Margarine
1 Tbsp Plain Flour
¼ Pt (75 ml) Red Wine
½ Tsp Dried Thyme
½ Ts Dried Rosemary

Slice the onions into thin rings, and place them in a saucepan with the butter. Cook over a medium heat for 7-10 minutes until softened.

Stir in the flour. Add the red wine slowly, stirring all the time to remove any lumps.

Add the herbs and seasoning and simmer for 5-10 minutes until thick and velvety.

This sauce is great with any kind of roast dishes.

Simple White Sauce

A great base for all sorts of sauces-once you've mastered this then the sky is your limit!

　　1 oz (25g) Butter or Margarine
　　2 Tbsp Plain Flour
　　½ Pt (150 ml) Milk
　　1 Tsp Vegetable Bouillon
　　Salt and Pepper

Melt the fat in a small saucepan over a low heat. Stir in the flour and cook, stirring constantly, for 2-3 minutes.

Gradually add the liquid and whisk while you bring it to the boil. Cook for 2–3 minutes, then remove from the heat and season to taste.

White Wine Variation
As above, but add ¼ Pt (75ml) white wine.

Cheese Variation
As above, but add 2 oz (50g) grated cheese and 1 Tsp Wholegrain Mustard.

Onion Variation
As above, but fry 1 small chopped onion in the first stage.

Homemade Honey Glaze Gravy

Similar to Red Wine Gravy but a much lighter sauce.

Serves 2
Leftover cooking Juices From Honey Glazed Carrots
1 Tbsp Plain Flour
½ Pt Vegetable Stock
1 Tsp Wholegrain Mustard
1 Tsp Fresh Coriander
Salt and Pepper

Place the leftover carrot liquid in a pan and gently heat. Slowly stir in the flour until the mixture has thickened, then add the stock a little at a time. You may have to use a whisk to avoid any lumps at this stage.

Stir in the mustard, salt and pepper and herbs. Cook on a low heat until sauce is thick and completely smooth.

Naam Prick

I discovered this amazing recipe in Thailand-its name literally means 'Spicy Water'!

Serves 2–4
4 Large Tomatoes
2-4 Small Red Chillies
Soy Sauce to taste
1 Tsp Brown Sugar
Water to thin

Cut the tomatoes in half and place them on a baking tray under a grill. Cook on a high heat until they bubble and the skins spilt.

Place the tomatoes and all their juices, with the remaining ingredients, into a food processor and blend until completely smooth.

This sauce is meant to be very thin and watery, so if yours is too thick then add extra soy sauce and a splash of water.

Best served drizzled over Congee (Page 74)

Leftovers Tip: Use any leftovers from this extremely hot sauce to spice up Thai Stir Fry or Coconut Curry-or just enjoy it added to other dishes to add a bit of a kick!

Simple Salad Dressing

This easy vinegarette is perfect for any salad.

2 Tbsp Olive Oil
2 Tbsp White Wine Vinegar
Chopped Fresh Herbs of Your Choice

Place all the ingredients into a clean jam jar and shake vigorously until completely blended. Pour over salad and toss well before serving.

Variations
    As above:
    … Add 1 Tsp of Peanut Butter
    … Add 2 crushed Garlic Cloves
    … Add 1 Tsp Clear Honey
    … Add ½ Tsp crushed dried Chillies
    … Add juice of 1 Lemon

Tzatziki

Serves 2-4 as Dip
1 Pot of Plain Yoghurt
½ Large Cucumber
1 Tbsp Mint

Chop the cucumber and mint, then mix all the ingredients together.
    For a more interesting version, try adding Crushed Garlic and Dried Chilli Powder.

Sweets For My Sweet

Bread and Butter Pudding

Coconut And Rosewater Custard

Summer Pudding

Apple and Blackberry crumble

Trifle

Mini Cakes

Banana Cake

Fruit Salad

Sweets For My Sweet

L AST BUT BY no means least – we have reached the Pudding Menu. What a wonderful way to round off any meal; a yummy sweet treat to fill that last corner.

Do you ever have the difficulty of the last "polite piece" of cake that no one will take? Well, here's an answer-instead of eating it to stop it from going to waste, or throwing it away because you're sick of the sight of it, why not make something completely new with it?

You can also use unexpected savouries as a base for your desserts-bread is a great one that can be surprisingly tasty, and a tiny bit healthier than some other puddings. So you can enjoy your sweets to your heart's content, minus the guilt!

Another tip to avoid those extra pounds whilst still giving in to your sweet craving is to swap cream or custard for low fat yoghurt or crème fraiche-equally delicious but minus a lot of the calories.

The following sweet recipes are ideal for using up ingredients that may be past their best, but you can also make them for their own right and enjoy them as they were meant to be enjoyed. Keep them as little nibbles for coffee time, or for an alternative, tasty meal finisher.

Bread and Butter Pudding

Serves 4-6
1 oz (25g) Butter
8 Slices Bread
2 oz (50g) Sultanas
12 fl oz Milk
3 ½ fl oz (100 ml) Cream
2 Eggs
1 oz Sugar
Grated Nutmeg

Grease a 1 pint pie dish. Remove crusts from the bread, butter one side and cut into triangles. Layer the bread, butter side up, in the pie dish. Sprinkle with a layer of sultanas. Repeat the layers until all the bread is used up.

Warm the milk and cream together over a high heat in a small pan. Beat the eggs together with ¾ of the sugar until the mixture is pale and thick. Pour this mixture over the bread layers. Sprinkle with the nutmeg and the last of the sugar and leave to stand for 30 minutes.

Bake in a preheated oven at Gas Mark 4 until set and golden on top. You can enjoy this lovely dessert hot or cold.

Coconut and Rosewater Custard

Serves 3–4
1 Packet Coconut Cream
¼ Pt (75ml) Water
2 oz (50g) Sugar
1 Tbsp Plain Flour
1 Tbsp Rose Water

Dissolve the coconut in the water and set over a low heat to simmer and thicken. Sift the flour into the mix to thicken further, whisk constantly at this stage to avoid lumps. Slowly stir in the sugar until it is all dissolved, then add the Rosewater.

Variations
Scrape the inside from a Vanilla pod and stir it into the pan in place of the Rosewater.

Replace the Rosewater with 1 Tsp Almond Essence.

Summer Pudding

This light dish is great for using up stale bread and an influx of berries!

Serves 4–6
6-8 Slices Old Bread (Crusts removed)
5 oz (125g) Caster Sugar
1 lb (500g) Mixed Summer Fruits (Blackberries, Strawberries, Raspberries)

Place the fruit and sugar in a large saucepan and heat gently, stirring frequently, until the sugar has dissolved and the fruit's juices start to run.

Line a large pudding bowl with the slices of bread (you can use more or less slices depending on the size of your bowl).

Spoon the fruit into the bow, and top with any remaining bread. Weigh down the pudding with a plate on top of it, and leave in the fridge for at least 8 hours.

Turn the pudding upside down and carefully remove the bowl. Serve with yoghurt or crème fraiche.

Apple And Blackberry Crumble

Serves 6–8

For The Crumble
8 oz (200g) Plain Flour
4 oz (100g) Butter or Margarine
1 oz (25g) Brown Sugar
1 Tbsp Mixed Dried Fruit

For The Filling
2 Large Cooking Apples
1 lb (500g) Blackberries
1 Tbsp Caster Sugar

Rub the flour and fat together until the mixture resembles fine bread-crumbs. Stir in the sugar and dried fruit.

Peel, core and roughly chop the apples. Place the blackberries, apples and sugar in a large saucepan over a low heat and simmer until the sugar has dissolved and the fruit has started to soften.

Grease a large, heatproof bowl and spoon in the fruit. Sprinkle the crumble topping over the fruit, and add 1–2 Tsp of brown sugar to make a caramelised top. Bake in the oven for 30 minutes until golden brown. Serve with frozen yoghurt.

Trifle

Serves 4–6
Leftover Sponge Cake
1 Packet Vegetarian Jelly
Coconut and Rosewater Custard (Page 101)
½ Pt (150ml) Double Cream
1 oz Dark Chocolate
¼ Pt Alcohol (this is optional, but if you do go for it,
    then I'd recommend Amaretto)
Icing Sugar to dust

Prepare the jelly according to instructions, and pour it into a deep dish. (If using alcohol, substitute the water for the alcohol). Break up the leftover cake and soak it in the jelly before it sets. Refrigerate until set.

Pour the rosewater custard over the jelly and cake mixture, and return to the fridge once it has cooled.

Whip the double cream until thick, then spoon over the rest of the mixture.

Decorate with grated chocolate.

Mini Cakes

This recipe is so simple it should hardly be called a recipe at all! But it deserves to be included as it is very good for avoiding waste.

Leftover Cake
Pastry Shape Cutters

Take your leftover cake and wrap it in tinfoil, then place it in a warm oven for 10 minutes (this will stop it from being hard and stale).

Using the pastry cutters, stamp out as many shapes as you can.

Dust with icing sugar and serve!

Banana Cake

Not only is this cake truly yummy, it i also great for using up bananas that no one in the house will eat-the blacker the better!

Serves 8-10
4 oz (100g) Butter or Margarine
10 oz (275g) Caster Sugar
12 oz (350g) Self Raising Flour
4 Ripe Bananas
3 fl oz (75ml) Milk
1 Tsp Honey
1 Tsp Vanilla Essence

Beat the butter and sugar together in a bowl until light and fluffy. Add the beaten eggs gradually to the mix.

In a separate bowl, sift together all the dry ingredients, then fold into the creamed mixture a little at a time. Stir well to ensure it is all blended together.

Mash the bananas into a paste, and add the milk, honey and vanilla essence. Mix until smooth, then fold into the cake mixture.

Divide the cake mixture between two 8 inch (20cm) cake tins, en-suring that you have first greased the tins with a little margarine.

Bake at Gas Mark 4 (180 C/350 F) for 30 minutes, until well risen and golden brown.

Allow to cool slightly before turning the cakes onto a wire rack. When completely cool, spread a thick layer of Raspberry Jam on one of the cakes, then place the other on top.

Fruit Salad

A fantastic recipe to use up fruit.

> *Serves 2–4*
> Fruit
> Juice of 1-2 Large Oranges
> Juice of ½ a Lemon
> ½ Tsp vanilla Essence

You can use any fruit you happen to have lying around for this recipe. Chop it all into small pieces and place in a bowl in the fridge.

Combine the fruit juices and pour over the chilled fruit. Serve cold.

Pickled Pink – Jams and Preserves

Onion Relish

Sweetcorn Relish

Marrow Chutney

Rhubarb Chutney

Apple Chutney

Pickled Onions

Pickled Beetroot

Piccalilli

Blackberry and Apple Jam

Raspberry Jam

Strawberry Jam

Plum Jam

Pickled Pink

THIS IS A chapter dedicated, not to leftovers, but to excess. What do you do with an overabundance of a certain vegetable or fruit? You preserve it, of course!

In the old days, preserving fruit and vegetables was the best way to keep and store them so that over the sparse winter months the family would have something to eat. Nowadays, with our fridge freezers and supermarkets that provide fresh fruit and veg the whole year round, this is less of a problem.

But still, it is a wonderful thing to open up a store cupboard and look in on rows of jars all filled with your very own homemade pickles, chutneys, jams and preserves. As well as being a cheap alternative to buying all of these things, it is very satisfying to know that you have bottled nutrition at your fingertips-all made by your own fair hand!

I am often stumped, especially at certain times of the year, about what to do with a sudden influx of, for example, courgettes, or runner beans. Being a country girl I grow lots of my own vegetables, and find that when it is time for harvesting, my beloved, carefully tended plants have come up trumps and yielded vast amounts of produce.

This is wonderful, of course, but there's is only so much room in a freezer, and because everyone else is growing the same vegetables I find I cannot even give them away to friends and neighbours, nor can I live on marrows alone!

All the following recipes are guaranteed favourites and are excellent ways of using up excesses of vegetables in a productive, healthy and tasty way. I have tried to include recipes which use the most prolific fruits and vegetables that many of us find in our gardens and allotments throughout the year.

Whether you are a spicy person or a sweet person, you will be able to find great tasting ways to preserve your produce within these pages. Don't worry if you don't grow your own however-these recipes can all be made with bought produce, and are great fun to make (and all are guaranteed to give you a glorious feeling of self righteous pride!)

Onion Relish

Makes about 12 jars
20 Medium Onions
2 Pints White Vinegar
1 lb (500g) Sugar
1 ½ Tsp Turmeric
1 ½ Tsp Mustard Seed
1 Tsp Celery Seed
Salt

Peel and slice the onions, making the slices very thin. Place some of the sliced onions into a large deep bowl, enough to cover the bottom, then sprinkle this with salt. Repeat with the remaining onions and as much salt is needed so that all the onions are coated. Cover the onions with water, then leave to stand overnight.

When the onions have soaked in the salt solution for around 24 hours, drain and wash them well to remove excess salt. Bring to boil the remaining ingredients, add the onions and boil for between five and eight minutes.

Pour the relish into warmed sterilised jars, leave to cool then cover and store.

Sweetcorn Relish

Makes 10 jars
10 oz (300g) White Cabbage
10 oz(300 g) Onions
6 Celery Stalks
2 Red Peppers
10 Corn Cobs (or 2 large tins of sweetcorn)
2 Pints (1.25 Litres) Cider Vinegar
1 lb(500g) Soft Brown Sugar
2-3 Tbsp Mustard Seed
1 Tbsp Salt

Finely chop the onions, celery and peppers (you can use a food processor for this). Place all the ingredients in a large saucepan. Bring to the boil, then simmer for 45 minutes to 1 hour, until the mixture is thick.

Pour the mixture into warmed sterilised jars, and pack down with a spoon to remove any air pockets. Cover and seal when the relish is cooled.

Marrow Chutney

Makes about 8 jars
4 lb (1.8 kg) Marrow
2 lb (900g) Onions
2 lb (900g) Tomatoes (Fresh or Tinned)
8 oz (225g) Sultanas
8 oz (225g) Brown Sugar
2 Pints (1.2 Litres) Malt Vinegar
2 Tsp Salt
1 Tsp Cayenne Pepper
1 ½ Tsp Pickling Spice

Peel the marrow and remove the cottony seeds. Chop into roughly 1 inch cubes. Peel and chop the onions, and the tomatoes (if using fresh).

Place all the ingredients into a large saucepan or preserving pan, bring to the boil slowly. Reduce the heat and simmer for about 2 hours, until the mixture is tender and reduced to a thick consistency.

Pour into warmed sterilised jars and leave to cool before covering and sealing. Store for 2-3 months to allow the flavours to mature.

Apple Chutney

Makes about 8 jars
4 lb (1.8kg) Apples
2 lb (900g) Onions
2 Tbsp Mustard Seed
Knob of Fresh Ginger (Or 2 Tsp Ground)
8oz (225g) Sultanas
1 lb (450g) Soft Brown Sugar
6 Chillies
1 ½ pint (900ml) Vinegar
1 Tbsp Salt

Chop the apples into large cubes and slice the onions. Finely chop the ginger (if using fresh). Place the mustard seeds in a heavy based pan over a high heat until they start to jump. Remove from the heat and grind them in a pestle and mortar or food processor.

Put all the ingredients in a large saucepan or preserving pan and cook for 1 ½-2 hours, until soft and pulpy.

Pour the chutney into warm sterilised jars, then allow to cool before covering and sealing the jars.

Rhubarb Chutney

Makes 8–10 jars
4 lb Rhubarb
1 lb (500 g) Brown Sugar
½ pint Cider Vinegar
½ oz (12g) Fresh or Dried Ginger
½ Tsp Cayenne Pepper
½ Tsp Salt
4 large Garlic Cloves
½ Tsp Ground Black Pepper

Finely chop the garlic and ginger (if using fresh) and add these to a pan with a tiny splash of oil. Cook on a very low heat until the garlic has softened.

Chop the rhubarb and add to the pan, stirring well. Add the vinegar and sugar and cook on a medium heat until soft.

Add the remaining ingredients and simmer until the mixture has reduced and thickened.

Allow to cool, then pour into warm sterilised jars, cover and seal.

Pickled Onions

Makes about 8 jars
2 ½ lb (1.25 kg) Small Onions
Salt
4 Tsp Mustard Seeds
2 Tsp Dill
Dried Chilli To Taste

Peel the onions but leave them whole. Place in a large bowl and cover with water. Drain off the water into a measuring jug, and add 2 oz (75g) of salt for every 1 ½ pints (1 Litre). Pour the salt and water over the onions, cover and leave to stand for 24 hours.

Rinse the onions well, and place them into a large sterilised jar (or several small jars) with the spices. Pour in enough vinegar to cover the onions, then drain out and boil the vinegar for 2 minutes.

Return the vinegar to the jar, ensuring the onions are covered by 1 inch (2.5 cm). Seal the jars and leave the onions to mature for around 4 weeks.

Pickled Beetroot

Makes 8–10 jars
2 ½ lb (1.25 Kg) Beetroot
2 Bay Leaves
2 Tsp Dried Cumin
4 Tsp Brown Sugar
Vinegar to cover

Boil the beetroot for 45 minutes-1 hour, until tender. Remove the skins by running the beetroot under a cold tap and rubbing the skin off. You can chop the beetroot into cubes, slices, or leave whole, if using baby beetroot.

Place the prepared beetroot into a large jar or several small ones, and pour in enough vinegar to cover. Drain the vinegar off and place into a large saucepan with the remaining ingredients. Boil for 2 minutes, then pour over the beetroot.

Allow to cool before covering and sealing the jars.

Piccalilli

Makes 8–10 jars
8oz (250g) Runner Beans
8oz (250g) Cauliflower
10oz (300g) Carrots
8oz (250g) Onions
1Lb (450g) Salt
8 Pints (4.5 Litres) Water
8oz (250g) Brown Sugar
2 Pints (1.2 Litres) White Vinegar
4 Tbsp Plain Flour
1 Tbsp Mustard Powder
1 Tbsp Ground Turmeric
½ Tsp Ground Ginger

Chop all the vegetables into bite sized pieces and set aside in a large bowl. Dissolve the salt in the water, and pour over the vegetables. Leave to soak for 24 hors.

Remove the vegetables from the brine and rinse well under cold water. Taste the veg, and if too salty then rinse again and leave to stand in cold water for 10 minutes before rinsing again.

Mix the sugar, mustard and ginger in a pan with 1 ½ pint of the vinegar. Add the vegetables and simmer for 20 minutes.

Blend the flour and turmeric with the remaining vinegar and stir into the vegetables. Boil for 1-2 minutes before pouring into warm sterilised jars. Leave to cool completely before covering and sealing.

A Quick Word On Jams...

A staple of most store cupboards, there is nothing like the deep, rich colours and sweet fruity taste of jam. You can use it to flavour rice puddings and yoghurt; you can make jam tarts; fill cakes-or just have jam on toast! Jam is a wonderful way to remind yourself of the glories of summer, and is the absolute best way to use up and store the abundance of autumn fruits.

Jam is not particularly difficult to make-though a word of warning should be given about the intense heat generated by cooking fruit and sugar. Make sure you are very careful with your jam cooking; do not allow any of it to touch bare skin as it will give you a very nasty burn-and try to ensure that no small children are running around as you prepare it as this can be a recipe for disaster.

Also, always ensure that you have warmed your jars before filling them with hot preserve-if you neglect to do this then the jars will crack and break. You can either place the jars in a hot oven for 10 minutes, or place them in boiling water before filling.

You will need a preserving pan or a large, deep, heavy based saucepan.

A wide mouthed funnel is another good investment as it will help you pour the jam from pan to pot with the minimum of spillage.

A thermometer is a handy tool to make sure your jam is getting up to temperature-in order to set perfectly, a jam should reach 105 C (221 F). If you do not have a thermometer then you can use the Wrinkle Test to check whether your jam has set: Spoon a small amount of jam onto a cold saucer and allow it to cool. Push a finger across the surface; if the jam is set then the surface will wrinkle.

Blackberry And Apple Jam

Makes 10–12 jars
4 lb (1.8Kg) Blackberries
1 ½ lb (700g) Apples
6 lb (2.7Kg) Sugar
½ pint (300ml) Water

Wash the blackberries and put them in a pan with ¼ pint (150ml) water. Simmer until soft.

Peel, core and slice the apples. Place in a preserving pan or large saucepan with the remaining water, and simmer until tender.

Add the cooked blackberries and sugar to the apple pulp, and stir over a gentle heat until the sugar has dissolved. Bring to the boil rapidly and boil, stirring frequently, until setting point is reached.

Pour the jam into warmed sterilised jars, cover and seal.

Raspberry Jam

Makes 6–8 jars
4 lb (1.8 kg) Raspberries
4 lb (1.8 kg) Sugar

Wash the raspberries, then place into a large pan and simmer slowly in their own juices for 15-20 minutes.

Add the sugar and stir until dissolved, then bring to the boil and continue boiling and stirring until setting point is reached.

Leave to cool for 15-20 minutes. Pour into warmed sterilised jars then cover and seal.

Strawberry Jam

Makes 8–9 jars
3 lb (1.6 kg) Strawberries
3 lb (1.6 kg) Sugar
3 Tbsp Lemon Juice

Wash and hull the strawberries. Put them in a preserving pan or large heavy saucepan with the lemon juice and simmer for 20-30 minutes until very soft.

Add the sugar and stir over a gentle heat until the sugar has dissolved.

Bring to the boil and continue to boil rapidly until setting point is reached.

Pour into warm sterilised jars and leave to cool for 15-20 minutes before covering and sealing.

Plum Jam

Makes 8–10 jars
6 lb (2.7 kg) Plums
6 lb (2.7 kg) Sugar
1 ½ pint (900ml) Water

Using a sharp knife, cut the plums in half and remove the stones. Crack open some of the stones and remove the kernels, and place these and the plums and water into a large pan and simmer until the fruit is soft.

Add the sugar and stir until dissolved. Bring to the boil and continue boiling until setting point is reached.

Leave to cool slightly, then pour into warm sterilised jars. Cover and seal.

Index

Lightning Source UK Ltd.
Milton Keynes UK
UKHW021036270819
348680UK00002B/3/P